KT-163-348

& Bat Bird

**ROD THEODOROU
AND
CAROLE TELFORD**

First published in Great Britain by Heinemann Library
Halley Court, Jordan Hill, Oxford OX2 8EJ
a division of Reed Educational & Professional Publishing Ltd

MELBOURNE AUCKLAND
FLORENCE PRAGUE MADRID ATHENS
SINGAPORE TOKYO CHICAGO SAO PAULO
PORTSMOUTH NH MEXICO
IBADAN GABORONE JOHANNESBURG
KAMPALA NAIROBI

© Heinemann Publishers (Oxford) Ltd 1996

Designed by Susan Clarke
Cover design by Simon Balley
Illustrations by Adam Abel
Printed in Great Britain by Bath Press Colourbooks, Glasgow

00 99 98 97 96
10 9 8 7 6 5 4 3 2 1

ISBN 0 431 06370 2

British Library Cataloguing in Publication Data
Theodorou, Rod
  Bat & bird. – (Spot the difference)
  1. Bats – Juvenile literature 2. Birds – Juvenile literature
  I. Title II. Telford, Carole
  598

Acknowledgements
The Publishers would like to thank the following for permission to reproduce photographs:
Nigel Tucker/Planet Earth Pictures p4; Hans Reinhard/Oxford Scientific Films p5 *left*; Kevin
Schafer/NHPA p5 *right*; John Downer/Planet Earth Pictures p6 *top*; Hans and Judy Beste/
Ardea London Ltd. pp3 *top*, 6 *bottom*, 12 *bottom*; Yuri Shibnev/Planet Earth Pictures p7;
Stephen Dalton/NHPA pp8, 16 *bottom*, Oxford Scientific Films p14; Gerard Lacz/NHPA p9;
I.R. Beames/Ardea London Ltd. p10; R. de la Harpe/Planet Earth Pictures p11 *top*; Mary
Clay/Planet Earth Pictures p11 *bottom*, Merlin Tuttle/Oxford Scientific Films pp12 *top*, 16 *top*;
A. Wharton/FLPA p13 *top*; Robert Tyrrell/Oxford Scientific Films pp3 *bottom*, 13 *bottom*, K.
Ammann/Planet Earth Pictures p15 *top*; Jan Johansson/Planet Earth Pictures p15 *bottom*; R.A.
Austing/FLPA p17; A.N.T./NHPA p18; Ken Lucas/Planet Earth Pictures p19, Ardea London
Ltd. p20; Michael Habicht/Oxford Scientific Films p21 *top*; Melvin Grey/NHPA p21 *bottom*;
Stephen Krasemann/NHPA, p22; David Hosking/FLPA p23

Cover photographs reproduced with permission of N.N. Birks/Ardea London Ltd. *top*;
Werner Curth/Ardea London Ltd. *bottom*

Every effort has been made to contact copyright holders of any material reproduced in this
book. Any omissions will be rectified in subsequent printings if notice is given to the Publisher.

Contents

Introduction

Only three kinds of animals can fly – bats, birds and insects. Bats are the only **mammals** that can fly. There are over 950 species of bat. They have small furry bodies and two leathery wings. Most bats are nocturnal. They sleep during the day and feed when the sun goes down at dusk.

It's amazing!
Most bats have tiny, weak legs. They can only crawl on the ground.

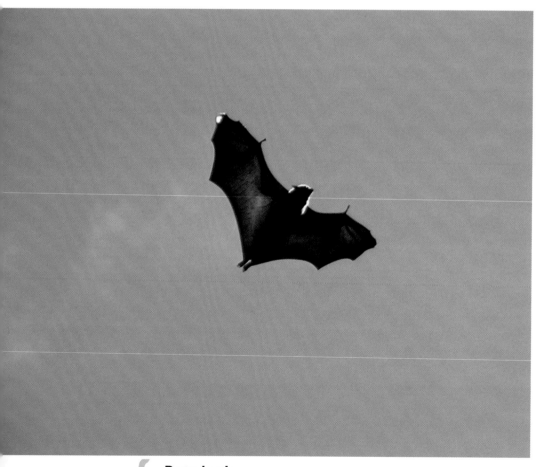

Bats look graceful when they fly, but not when they stop.

Starlings are one of the most common birds in the world.

Penguins have thick feathers to protect them from the cold of the Antarctic.

There are over 9000 **species** of bird. Birds are the only animals that grow feathers to keep themselves warm and dry. They have beaks, wings and strong legs to hold onto branches or to hop along the ground. Some birds, like ostriches, emus and penguins, cannot fly.

Where they live

Bats live in many parts of the world. They sleep in places where they will not be disturbed during the day. They **roost** in caves, trees and old buildings. Bats which live in cooler countries **hibernate** during the winter. Many types of bat are becoming rarer because their **habitats** are being destroyed.

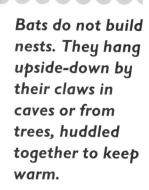

Bats do not build nests. They hang upside-down by their claws in caves or from trees, huddled together to keep warm.

It's amazing!

Some bats migrate to warmer countries. Some migrate over 1000 kilometres, flying over 50 kilometres a day!

Birds live all over the world, from frozen Antarctica to dry, hot deserts and tropical rainforests. Half of all the different species **migrate** once a year to find a better place to breed. When it is time to lay their eggs, birds make a nest in a safe place. Over 1000 species of bird are in danger of **extinction** because of pollution, hunting, or the destruction of their **habitats**.

The golden eagle can make a nest as wide as a car!

Wonderful wings

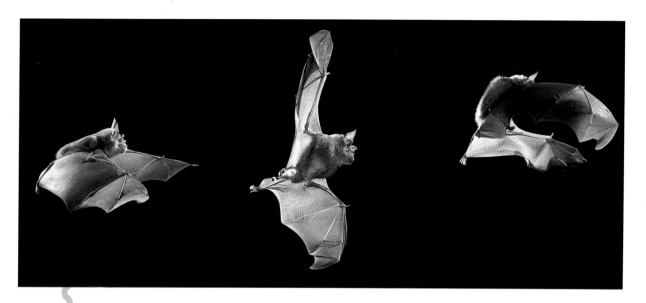

A bat in flight.

Bats fly with their hands! They have long arms and very long finger bones. Thin leathery skin grows across these bones, like material on an umbrella. The thumb is short and has a useful claw to help the bat climb or grip its food. Bats have strong chest and shoulder muscles to help them fly.

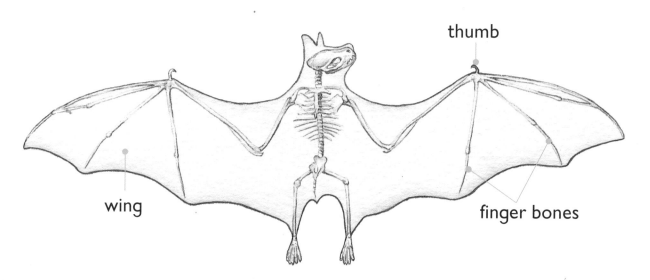

thumb

wing

finger bones

The skeleton of a bat.

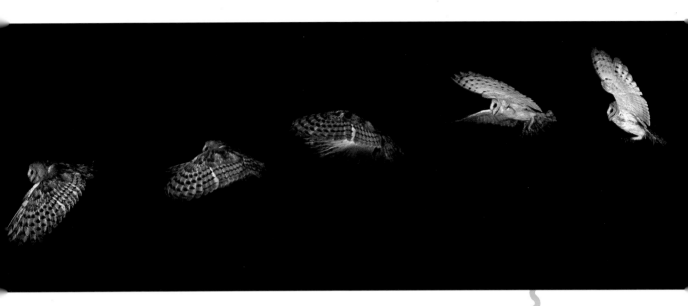

Birds are the fastest and most powerful flying animals. Their wings are curved on top and flat underneath, like the wings of a plane. Their bones are hollow and light. They have a large breastbone and powerful chest muscles to help them fly. Small birds can flap their wings fast and twist and turn through the trees. Large birds can spread their wings and soar across mountains and oceans.

It's amazing!

Birds' feathers are made from keratin, the same as your hair and nails.

An owl in flight.

The skeleton of a bird.

wing

breastbone

Senses

Some people think that bats are blind. This is not true. Bats have good eyesight, but many of them need to be able to fly and catch **prey** in total darkness. To do this they have developed **echo** location. The bat makes a high-pitched squeak. The sound bounces off objects and echoes back to the bat. Different things make different echoes. By listening to the echoes bats can even find and catch tiny moths in the dark.

It's amazing!

Many bats have huge ears to help hear the echos. The long-eared bat has ears that are almost as long as its body!

Most fruit bats do not use echo location. This bat uses its big eyes and long nose to find ripe fruit and flowers.

Birds have a poor sense of smell, but good eyesight. Eagles and hawks have eyesight twice as good as ours, to spot small animals below them as they fly. Most birds have good hearing and will often sing to let other birds know where they are. Birds also sing to attract a mate. At breeding time, some birds sing their song over a thousand times a day!

A vulture looking for dead or dying animals to feed on.

Owls have good eyesight and hearing. They need it to catch mice rustling through the grass at night.

Plant-eaters

This fruit bat is eating bananas.

Lesser long-nosed bat about to feed.

Fruit-eating bats are often called flying foxes. They only live in hot countries. They eat fruit like bananas, mangoes and guavas. They also lick **nectar** and **pollen** from flowers. Sometimes pollen gets stuck on their fur and is carried to other flowers. This helps new flowers to grow in other places. Fruit bats help fruit trees to grow too, because seeds are spat out, or are in their droppings.

Many birds eat fruit, seeds or other plants. Seed-eating birds often have thick, strong beaks to crack open nuts and pine cones. Birds that eat water plants often have flat bills, like ducks. Many plant-eating birds live in towns and cities, finding their food in gardens or parks.

Starlings are very common birds. As well as fruit they will eat insects and seeds.

It's amazing!

Hummingbirds have thin bills and long tongues which they use like a straw, to suck nectar from flowers.

Insect-eaters

Most bats are insect-eaters. They use **echo** location to hunt moths, gnats and mosquitoes. They catch them in their mouths or scoop them up in the flap of skin between their legs, or in their wings. Some bats even pluck spiders off their webs.

It's amazing!

Some moths can hear the high-pitched squeak that bats make when they are hunting. The moths stop flying and drop to the ground to avoid being caught and eaten.

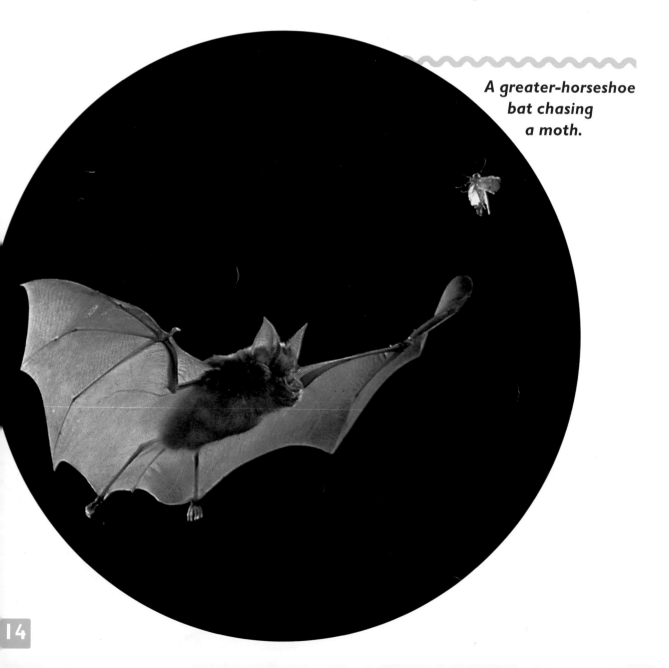

A greater-horseshoe bat chasing a moth.

Insect-eating birds often have thin, pointed beaks. Some catch insects in the air. Others look on the ground or on the bark of trees to find hidden beetles or grubs. Bee-eaters catch bees and squeeze out the bee sting before they eat them. Flamingos sieve tiny creatures from the water. Their long legs help to keep their feathers dry.

A flamingo feeding on creatures found in shallow water.

This nuthatch is looking for beetles and earwigs in the tree bark.

Meat-eaters

Some bats use **echo** location to catch fish! When a small fish swims close to the surface of the water, fish-eating bats can detect the ripples and swoop down to catch the fish. Other big bats, like the false vampire bat, will eat frogs, rodents, lizards, small birds and even other bats.

A fisherman bat catching a fish while in flight.

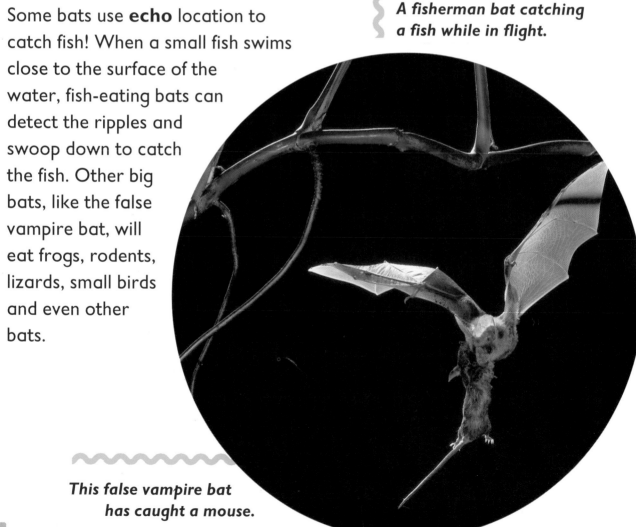

This false vampire bat has caught a mouse.

Fish-eating birds, like herons and kingfishers, have sharp bills to stab their prey. Birds of prey, like eagles, hawks and owls, have huge hooked claws and beaks for gripping and tearing flesh. The African harrier hawk has specially flexible legs to help it to reach into holes in trees to grab nesting birds or bats. Owls will eat bats if they can catch them.

A saw-whet owl swooping to catch a mouse.

Babies

Female bats look for a warm, dry **roost** when it is time to have their babies. Thousands of females huddle together in the same place, often giving birth at exactly the same time. Most bats only have one baby a year. Insect-eating bats are born blind and without fur. Fruit bats are born with their eyes open.

It's amazing!

Mother bats, returning to the nursery roost, find their own baby by smell and echo location.

Eastern horseshoe bats in a nursery roost.

Most birds build a nest in which the eggs are laid. Some birds lay just one egg. Others can lay as many as nineteen. The parents sit on the eggs to keep them warm until they hatch – this is called incubation. Some birds' eggs need about 11 days to hatch, while others need up to 80 days.

Chicks are born with a special 'egg-tooth' to help them to break out of their egg.

Growing up

Mother bats feed their babies milk. When the mother flies off to find food the babies huddle together to keep warm. After one to three months the baby bats are ready to fly. Young bats have to practice **echo** location and sometimes fly behind their mother to learn how to hunt.

It's amazing!

Baby fruit bats sometimes hang from branches and flap their wings to practice flying!

Baby birds are called nestlings. The parents fly off and hunt for food for them until the babies are old enough to fly. Birds that are old enough to leave the nest and begin to learn to fly and feed themselves are called **fledgelings**. Many clumsy fledgelings are caught by birds of prey.

Nestlings open their mouths wide to show their parents that they need feeding.

A barn owl brings a rabbit back for its young.

Fact file

Bat

Largest
The wingspan of a bismark flying fox can be as long as 183 cm – as long as a human is tall.

Smallest
Kitti's hog-nosed bat has a wingspan of only 16 cm.

Fastest
The Mexican free-tailed bat can fly at 51 kph.

Food
Plant-eaters eat fruit, pollen and nectar.

Insect-eaters eat gnats, mosquitoes, dragonflies, moths and also grasshoppers, crickets and spiders.

Meat-eaters eat frogs, fish, rodents, birds and other bats.

A colony of bats in Bracken Cave, Texas.

Life span
Most bats live from 5 to 20 years. There is a record of a banded little brown bat living to the age of 32.

Largest colony
One colony of Mexican free-tailed bats (in Bracken Cave, Texas, USA) was estimated to have 20,000,000 bats in one cave!

Bird

The ostrich is one of the species of bird which cannot fly.

Largest

The ostrich can grow up to 2.74 m tall and weigh 156.5 kg.

The largest flying birds are bustards, which can weigh up to 18 kg.

Largest wing span: the albatross has a wing span of up to 3.63 m.

Smallest

The bee hummingbird is only 6 cm long and weighs 1.6 g.

Fastest

The peregrine falcon can swoop at speeds of up to 270 kph.

Food

Some birds eat only seeds, fruit or insects. Some, like crows, also eat worms and dead meat. Many seabirds eat mainly fish. Small birds of prey catch mice and other small animals. The biggest birds of prey will catch animals as big as a young deer.

Life span

'Cocky', a cockatoo at London Zoo, lived for 80 years.

Largest colony

One flock of red-billed queleas (living in the Sudan) had 32,000,000 birds in it!

Glossary

echo a sound that bounces back.

extinction when all the animals of a species die out.

habitats the place in which an animal lives.

hibernate to sleep through winter.

mammals animals covered in fur that feed their young with milk.

migrate to move from one area to another each year.

nectar a sweet liquid like honey that some plants make to attract birds, bats and insects.

pollen tiny yellow grains produced by male parts of plants which fertilise the female parts.

prey an animal that is hunted by another for food.

roost the place a flying animal sleeps.

species a group of living things that are very similar.

Index